A Personal Tour of
MESA VERDE

ROBERT YOUNG

LERNER PUBLICATIONS COMPANY ▪ MINNEAPOLIS

Cover: *Residents of Balcony House spent much of the day on the plazas that fronted the dwellings. Plazas served as places to cook, to sew, to grind corn, to eat, and to socialize.*
Title page: *An illustration reveals what a slice of life at Cliff Palace may have looked like. Each pueblo was a sprawling structure with many rooms and many levels. The sizes of ancient Puebloan villages are determined by the number of rooms instead of separate buildings.*

Many thanks to the dedicated staff of Mesa Verde National Park, particularly Larry Wiese, Sarah Craighead, and Lucy Lynch; to Katy Holmgren for her editorial support; and to Sara Young and Tyler Young for their curiosity and continued interest in *How It Was.*

For Lucy Lynch, an outstanding tour guide

Website address: www.lernerbooks.com

LIBRARY OF CONGRESS CATALOGING-IN-PUBLICATION DATA

Young, Robert, 1951–
  A personal tour of Mesa Verde / by Robert Young
    p. cm.—(How it was)
  Includes index.
  Summary: Presents a tour of the Anasazi cliff dwellings in Colorado through the eyes of some of the people who lived and visited there nearly 800 years ago.
  ISBN 0-8225–3577–7 (lib. bdg. : alk. paper)
  1. Pueblo Indians—Antiquities—Juvenile literature. 2. Mesa Verde National Park (Colo.)—Juvenile literature. 3. Cliff-dwellings—Colorado—Juvenile literature. 4. Colorado—Antiquities—Juvenile literature.
[1. Pueblo Indians. 2. Indians of North America—Southwest, New.
3. Mesa Verde National Park (Colo.) 4. Cliff-dwellings—Southwest, New.
5. Colorado—Antiquities.] I. Title. II. Series
E99.P9Y68 1999
978.8'01—dc21   98–9422

Manufactured in the United States of America
1 2 3 4 5 6 – JR – 04 03 02 01 00 99

Contents

High, flattopped mesas rise from the surrounding area of deep canyons and steep cliffs.

One might regard architecture as history
arrested in stone. —A.L. Rowse

Introduction

Mesa Verde sits in the southwestern corner of the state of Colorado in the southwestern United States. A mesa is a raised area of land with a flat top and steep sides. In Spanish the word *mesa* means "table," and *verde* means "green." Spaniards named this area Mesa Verde because of its shape and because of the green color of the trees and bushes that grow on the mesa top.

Millions of years of wind, rain, and running streams have eroded the sides of the mesa. These actions riddled the **sandstone cliffs** with shallow caves and created ledges with rock overhangs. A group of Native Americans— known as the **ancient Puebloans**—had been living in villages (pueblos) on top of the mesa since about A.D. 550. There they farmed corn, squash, and beans. Around the year 1200, some ancient Puebloans decided to build villages in the shallow caves of the cliff faces.

Why build a village in the side of a cliff? No one knows the answer to this question. Scientists have many different theories. Maybe the cliff dwellers needed more of the mesa top for farmland. Maybe they wanted protection from the weather or from their enemies. Some scientists believe that a group of religious Puebloans who wanted privacy lived in the cliff villages.

The villages in the cliffs of Mesa Verde vary in size. Some contain only a few rooms. Cliff Palace, the largest village, is made up of more than 100. Balcony House, built on a ledge only 400 feet long, has about 45 rooms. Situated at the southern end of Mesa Verde, Balcony House faces eastward into Soda Canyon. Unlike most cliff towns, it had a spring that provided fresh water to the residents.

Cliff Palace (left) *is the largest site at Mesa Verde. A map* (facing page) *shows an overview of Mesa Verde National Park. The white shading represents canyons, which vein the landform. The mesa, in beige, housed ancient Puebloans before some built cliff dwellings. An inset map shows the park in context with the surrounding territory.*

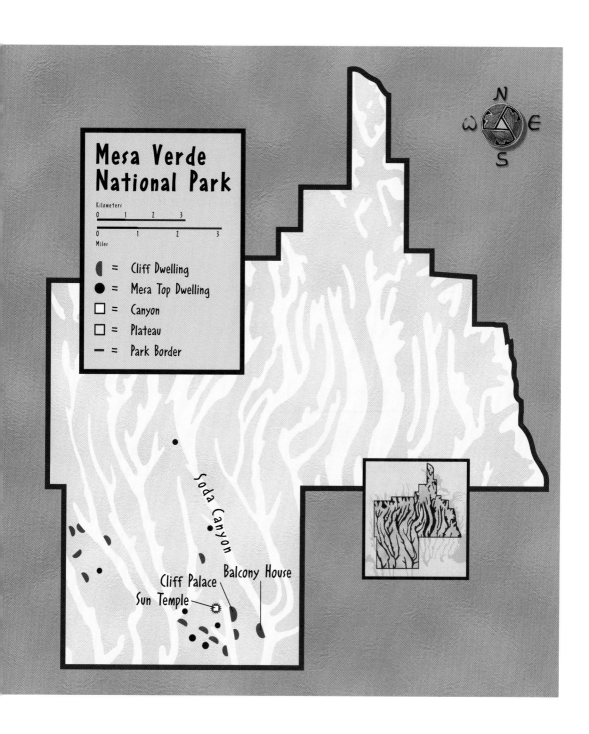

Mesa Verde National Park

Kilometers
0   1   2   3

0   1   2   3
Miles

◗ = Cliff Dwelling
● = Mesa Top Dwelling
☐ = Canyon
☐ = Plateau
— = Park Border

Soda Canyon

Balcony House

Cliff Palace

Sun Temple

Because Balcony House has such a steep slope from back to front, the ancient Puebloans carved handholds and toeholds to make the passage to the alcove easier to use. Similar holds are found on the cliff face.

Balcony House could be reached only by climbing 30 feet down a steep cliff. The ancient Puebloans—expert climbers—had made this possible by carving handholds and toeholds into the sandstone cliff. They also created a 12-foot-long tunnel that had to be crawled through to enter or leave the village. Why did the ancient Puebloans make it so hard to get to Balcony House? No one knows. Farmers, hunters, and others may have had to enter and exit the town nearly every day. In the winter, ice and snow could have kept the people of Balcony House captive in their village.

The people of Balcony House filled the naturally uneven ledge with stones to make it level to build on. Most buildings rose two stories. They overlooked two **plazas** (separated from one another by a high wall) and faced the canyon. The cliff dropped sharply in front of the village but then sloped to the canyon far below. Only by walking behind the buildings, along the inside of the cave, could a Puebloan travel from one side of the village to the other. A spring was against the back of the alcove, as was a trash heap.

We'll be taking a closer look at Mesa Verde. Imagine it's a chilly, late fall morning in the year 1250 at Balcony House...

A carefully crafted tunnel provided entrance to Balcony House. Experts have not determined why the ancient Puebloans would have built this elaborate entryway.

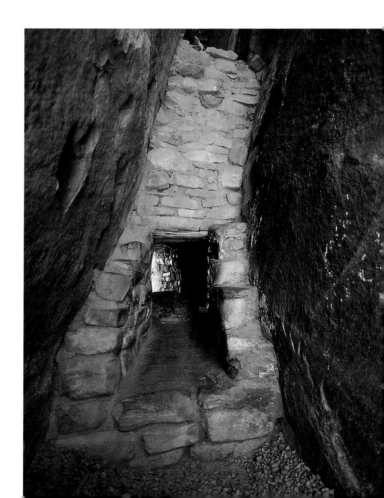

Balcony House, a medium-sized cliff village, sits in a shallow cave about 600 feet above the floor of Soda Canyon.

They were a . . . people with roots wound
deep in generations of life upon the land . . .
moving in harmony to the . . . order that nature
laid down with the seasons. —Donald G. Pike

With East Wind

East Wind opened her eyes in the small stone room and saw light from the rising sun shining through the doorway. She pulled the feather blanket up around her neck to keep warm and took a deep breath of cold air that smelled like earth and smoke. Her husband, Blue Corn, slept soundly beside her. East Wind started to wake him but then remembered that the harvest was over. He could sleep a little longer today.

The second-story room measured eight feet long, six feet wide, and five-and-one-half feet high. It was about the same size as the other rooms at Balcony House. Like most of the other people who lived at Mesa

No one knows what names the ancient Puebloans had. Their descendants—the Hopis and other Pueblo peoples—have names that, translated into English, are close to the ones in this book.

Verde, East Wind was about five feet tall, so she could stand up without feeling cramped. The floor was made of packed dirt, and the brick walls were coated with plaster.

East Wind and her husband used this second-story room for sleeping and for storing blankets, sleeping mats, and clothes.

The sleeping mat made of willow boughs creaked as East Wind got off of it. She slid her feet into her yucca sandals and pulled a cotton blanket around her shoulders. Stepping to the fire pit, she chose a piece of juniper bark from the pile. She crumbled it and put pieces onto the embers that were still warm from last night's fire. She blew on the embers until they glowed bright red, and sparks jumped out to light the bark. East Wind added juniper wood as the fire grew.

Yucca *(Yucca baccata)* was one of the most important plants for the ancient Puebloans. They made soap out of the yucca roots and made mats and baskets from its leaves. Craftspeople twisted the strong fibers in the leaves into ropes and cords or used the fibers as paintbrushes. The ancient Puebloans liked to eat the fruit baked or boiled. People munched on toasted yucca seeds or ground them into flour.

As East Wind warmed her hands over the fire, she heard the familiar sounds of the village. Her neighbors were doing their morning chores. Pet turkeys chattered as they roamed through the streets, and dogs barked and played.

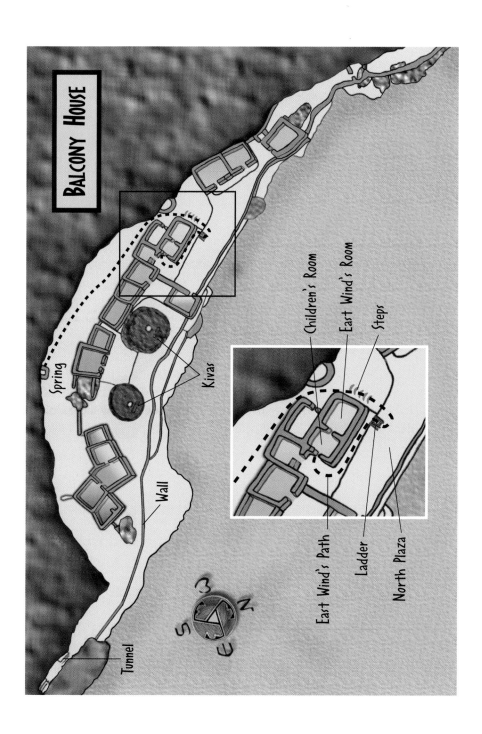

BALCONY HOUSE

Children's Room

East Wind's Room

Steps

Spring

Kivas

Wall

East Wind's Path

Ladder

North Plaza

Tunnel

Taking her broom of stiff grass from its place against the wall, East Wind quietly swept the dirt floor of the small stone room. Then she carefully arranged her extra clothes in a pile in the corner. East Wind owned her family's house. She worked very hard to keep it neat and clean.

East Wind stood close to the wall and examined it. Last spring she'd used mud and small stones to fill some cracks between the sandstone bricks. This coming spring she'd have to replace the whole wall. Last year Blue Corn had helped her take down a different wall, which they'd rebuilt stone by stone. It had taken time—hours they could have spent at work. East Wind thought the repairs would last through the winter because no cracks had appeared yet in the plaster that covered the wall.

Most scientists believe that women owned the homes at Balcony House and that inheritance was figured through the woman's side of the family. When people married, the couple built another room onto the wife's parents' house. Sisters and their husbands would add rooms, too. If the new husband did not like this, or if his in-laws did not like him, he would go and live in his mother's house.

East Wind climbed through the small, T-shaped doorway. Its narrow bottom and wide top reduced drafts and also made it easier to defend the rooms from intruders while allowing people with packs on their backs to pass through. The T shape created ledges in the door that could be used as handholds for people climbing into a room from a ladder. East Wind stepped onto the narrow balcony formed by jutting roof beams that also supported her second-story sleeping room.

The T-shaped doorways (left) *served many useful purposes.* (Above) *In building the walls, each sandstone brick had to be carefully shaped and laid. Mortar secured the bricks in place.*

After walking along the balcony, East Wind peeked through the tiny window of the next sleeping room. Raven Feather, her younger son, and Light Cloud, her daughter, were still asleep on their mats. Her older son, Fast River, spent most nights at the kiva (an underground ceremonial room), where he was learning the skills of a priest.

East Wind decided not to wake the children yet. She squinted across the canyon to look at the sunrise and inhaled the crisp air. Winter would soon come to the mesa, but until then East Wind would enjoy fall, her favorite time of year. She loved the season's rituals and ceremonies, such as the harvest celebration.

She looked down into Soda Canyon at the trees flecked with red, yellow, orange, and green. She scanned the village, noticing the harvested crops drying in the open air. She saw the yellow and white corncobs hanging from the roof poles of the houses. Kernels of red, black, blue, and speckled corn had been spread over the rooftops to dry.

Piles of brown beans and yellow squash lay in the corners of the two plazas—open areas in front of the buildings where people sat to eat meals, to relax, to grind corn, and to sew. The two plazas stretched along the ledge, separating the buildings from Soda Canyon.

East Wind climbed down a wooden ladder to North Plaza and paused to listen for sounds of her mother, Corn Woman. The older woman had lived alone after East Wind's father died two years before. East Wind heard the sound of a broom whisking across the floor. Although she was old, Corn Woman still rose at dawn.

East Wind smiled as she lifted a large pottery jug that

Food production and preparation occupied many hours each day. Corn was the primary food source. Over time farmers bred different colors and varieties of corn.

Corrugated, or roughened, jars are commonly found artifacts in Mesa Verde. The pinched coils made the sturdy jars easy to grip, and yucca-fiber mats could keep them steady on the ground.

sat near her mother's door. She was glad that the jug had carefully roughened sides that made it easy to grip. Carrying the empty jug under her arm, East Wind crossed the plaza, climbed some steps, and walked behind the village buildings. Here the cave's roof sloped down to meet its floor.

The spring was against the back of the alcove. Water seeped through the sandstone, collecting in a small pool. It provided fresh, clean water for everyone in the village to drink and cook with. Not many of the cliff villages had such good supplies of water. East Wind knew that her village was lucky.

Other women were already kneeling near the cool water. This was a good place to catch up on the village

Dwellers of Balcony House were lucky to have a supply of fresh water within their walls. Gathering water was probably part of the daily routine.

news. As she used a dried squash shell to ladle water into her jug, East Wind chatted and listened. One woman said that a trader was coming to the village soon. East Wind hoped he would be bringing cotton with him. Blue Corn needed more of the soft fiber to finish the warm blankets for the cold winter ahead.

Finally the jug was full. East Wind lifted it onto her head. Luckily she'd remembered to bring a ring of yucca fibers to place between the jug and her hair to protect her head from the hard jug. It was a short walk back to North Plaza.

Sunlight filled the plaza, and several people were already at work. East Wind greeted her mother and her daughter who were kneeling in a corner of the plaza. Corn Woman was preparing to help Light Cloud and other young girls grind corn.

Blue Corn sat nearby in the plaza. His large hands moved slowly as he carefully wrapped fluffy turkey feathers tightly around cords of yucca. Later he would weave the long cords into a soft, warm blanket.

Some men made turkey-feather blankets for people in the village. Others used cotton to weave blankets or ceremonial garb. The ancient Puebloans made clothes from the skins of deer and mountain sheep that workers had tanned into soft leather. They used tools of bone to sew the skins into robes, leggings, and jackets.

Before starting her sewing for the day, East Wind decided to check on her younger son. She climbed the ladder and looked into the room where Raven Feather had been sleeping. She smiled when she saw his empty mat. The boy was up and already at work. East Wind was glad that all of her family helped out.

Large plazas in front of the buildings provided gathering places. The circular kivas were topped with wooden coverings, which also served as the floor of the plaza.

The ancient Puebloans often stored corn in black-and-white earthenware pots. The elegant pottery was also used for cooking and for decoration.

Treat your corn as lovingly as you would treat your child. —Old Pueblo saying

With Light Cloud

Light Cloud knelt in the corner of the plaza. Its flat rocks felt cool under her knees. Corn Woman, her grandmother, stood over her. Two other girls from the village were there, one on each side of Light Cloud. All three of the girls were nine years old.

A sandstone slab, called a **metate,** sat in front of each girl. The high ends of the metates faced the girls, so that the stones sloped downward to the ground. Corn Woman placed a clay bowl near the low end of each metate and nodded. It was time to grind corn.

Corn, usually in the form of cornmeal, was the foundation of ancient Puebloan cooking. Mixed with water, cornmeal was cooked in many different ways. It could be baked in small cakes, baked in corn husks, or rolled into little balls and boiled. Young women probably ground cornmeal by hand every day.

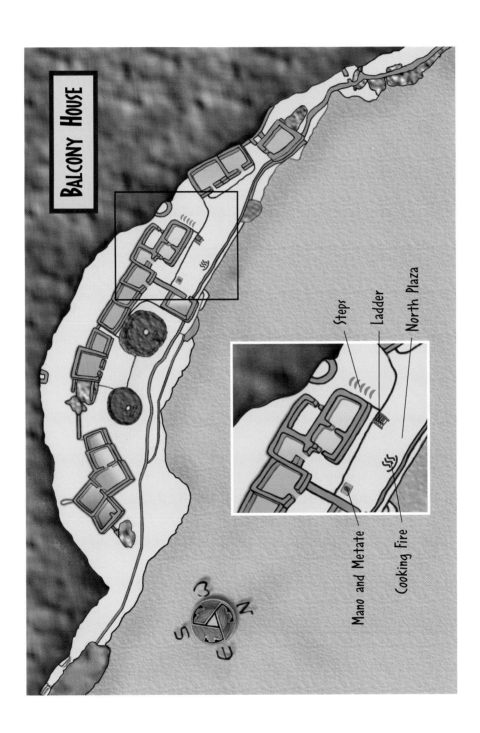

BALCONY HOUSE

Steps

Ladder

North Plaza

Mano and Metate

Cooking Fire

A mano and metate were used to grind cornmeal (above). *The cornmeal was put through the grinding process three times* (inset).

The three girls were working together under Corn Woman's watchful eye. The girl to Light Cloud's right began the process by spreading a handful of dried corn kernels on her metate. With a hard, heavy rock called a **mano,** she ground the kernels into fragments. Then Corn Woman helped by sweeping the cracked corn into a wide, flat basket with low sides. She shook it, and the light-weight hulls (outer coverings) floated away on the wind. The corn itself was left behind in the basket.

Light Cloud's job was to grind this broken corn into smaller pieces. Then she would pass the crushed corn to the last girl, who would finish the process by grinding the cornmeal into a fine powder.

Light Cloud gripped a mano with both hands and leaned forward as she rubbed the stone across the hulled corn. Caught between the mano and the metate, the fragments jumped and bumped. The other girls also moved their manos back and forth. As the three sang a song about the harvest, the bits of corn were pushed down the sloping metate and into the clay bowls. Light Cloud felt her hands getting sweaty and changed her hold on the heavy mano. It was a valuable one that a trader had brought from a place with many hard rocks. Compared to this mano, the sandstone of the metate seemed soft. In fact, the mano had worn a trough in the stone.

Some scientists believe that eating cornmeal wore down the teeth of ancient Puebloans. Part of the problem had to do with the processing method. Each time the corn was ground on the metate, grit became mixed with the corn. The grit-and-cornmeal combination was eaten at every meal.

The girls pushed their manos, in unison, along the metates. Every morning they spent two or three hours grinding the day's corn. As the girls worked, Corn Woman told stories about the corn gods and taught songs to make the work go more quickly.

Still singing and grinding, Light Cloud saw her grandmother walk across the plaza to the nearest cooking fire and add more wood to it. The older woman had been stoking the fire since early morning, keeping it very hot by adding more and more wood. A large clay pot filled with boiling water sat on a flat rock in the middle of the fire. Smoke, mixed with the sweet smell of ground corn, rose from the fire and drifted toward the girls.

Light Cloud watched Corn Woman scoop up some of the fresh cornmeal, add water to it, and shape it into small balls. She carried the cornmeal balls to the pot and dropped them into the boiling water. The midday meal would be a larger one than usual, since Trader was arriving soon. Light Cloud's mother planned to invite him

One of the sweetest foods the ancient Puebloans ate was corn bread made with saliva (spit). To make this bread, young women chewed the cornmeal until their saliva changed the corn's natural starch into sugar. The chewed meal was mixed with the rest of the cornmeal and baked to make a sweet bread. This bread was a special food served to honored guests.

to share the family's midday meal. Light Cloud wished they'd known earlier that Trader was coming, because then she could have helped make sweet corn bread for him. Regular corn bread would have to do.

When the three girls finished singing a corn song, Light Cloud was surprised to see that the sun had risen high in the sky. It was already noon, and the day's corn was nearly ground! She was always surprised at how quickly the time passed.

Light Cloud was happy that she was old enough for the task of grinding corn and that her arms and shoulders were growing strong. She'd helped her father plant the corn on top of the mesa in early May, when the ground was still wet from the melted snow. Blue Corn had used a stone-tipped digging stick to make a hole in the soil and then had let Light Cloud drop the seeds into the holes.

Scientists believe that ancient Puebloan men owned the farm fields. Although everyone probably helped out, men are thought to have done most of the farming. In addition to growing corn, the ancient Puebloans raised beans and squash. Farmers planted squash in the same fields as the corn. Squash plants shaded the ground with large, flat leaves. Beans might have been started on trays inside the pueblos—perhaps in the kivas—and transferred to gardens when they were sturdy. Some Zuni farmers *(pictured above)*, members of a modern-day Pueblo people, continue to use many of these traditional planting methods.

Planting the corn was very important, so she hadn't been allowed to help too much. It was really Blue Corn's work.

Light Cloud remembered how glad she'd been when the spring rains had kept the plants alive through the long, dry summer. As the corn grew, Blue Corn and the other farmers had spent their days weeding and protecting the plants. Light Cloud had worked hard picking off bugs and, with her brother Raven Feather, had pretended to be a hunter as she chased birds, squirrels, rabbits, and deer away from the fields. Most village children had helped out in this way. Some men had camped near the fields to guard the crops all night long.

Every year farmers worried about the crop until August, when it was harvesttime. At this time of year, heavy rain fell on the mesa top. If the rain came too early, it would damage the young plants. Every day from August until October, the villagers picked the mature corn and carried it back to the village, where the harvest was then dried and stored. Light Cloud could hardly believe that the corn kernels she had helped plant were already being dried. The long, hot summer had gone by quickly!

A desert cottontail rabbit is among the animals able to survive the harsh seasons of the Southwest.

Mule deer roam the mesa. Ancient Puebloan hunters relied on this animal for meat, bones, and leather.

Corn grows in our fields,
Deer run on the mountains,
The snow melts into the rivers,
And the clouds gather to bring us rain.

—Alice Marriot

With Trader

Trader walked along the trail that crossed the mesa. On his shoulders rested a large deer-hide pack filled with shells, cotton, salt, and turquoise (a blue stone) to trade. Although the air was still cool, walking had kept him warm. It was just past noon, and he'd been walking since leaving a village on the mesa soon after sunrise.

Trader saw some chokecherry bushes and picked a few of the small, black berries to eat. Sniffing the air, he smelled the fresh scent of sagebrush. He noticed that a deer eating leaves from a nearby fendlerbush froze as he approached. He stood very still. When the deer began to chew again, Trader quietly continued along the trail.

The scent of sagebrush gave way to the familiar odor of smoke. Trader looked down into the canyon. No sign of smoke there! He looked northward across the bushes and saw plumes of gray against the blue sky. He guessed that farmers were burning off trees and bushes to make room for more fields.

Trader recognized the twists of the path and knew the next village on his journey was close by. Soon he would come to the edge of the mesa where he would have to travel down part of the cliff to reach the village. Despite his heavy bag and tired legs, Trader ran swiftly along the trail. Small puffs of dust rose as his feet pounded the earth.

It wasn't long before Trader came to a sudden stop. Before him lay the end of the trail—and Soda Canyon! Trader took a deep breath and admired the view, trying to forget that he had almost run right off the edge of the mesa. He had passed his destination. He walked back and found the right trail. Seemingly from nowhere, a guard appeared in front of him. The young man held a bow and arrow threateningly until he recognized Trader.

The mesa drops off sharply, forming canyons. The soft sandstone wore away over thousands of years.

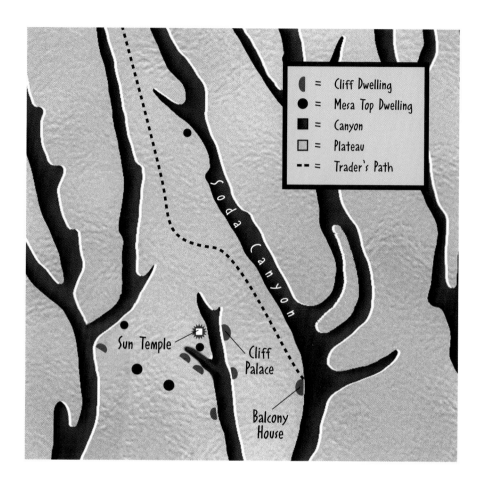

They exchanged greetings, and the guard handed Trader a length of yucca-fiber rope. Trader tied one end of the rope to his pack and then carefully lowered the heavy bag to a narrow ledge below. Next he began to climb down the cliff using the handholds and toeholds the villagers had carved into the rock.

Slowly and carefully, Trader worked his way down the cliff. He didn't want to slip. Falling to the canyon below could injure him badly—maybe even kill him.

Barefoot or wearing sandals, ancient Puebloans were skillful climbers who used cracks in the rock and carefully carved handholds and toeholds.

When Trader reached the three-foot-wide ledge, he untied the rope, which the guard pulled back up. Trader lifted his pack, glanced at Soda Canyon gaping to his right, and moved along the ledge until he met a second guard. With a friendly nod, this guard stepped away from a dark hole—the mouth of a tunnel. Trader placed his pack at the tunnel's mouth and pushed it along as he crawled after it. The smooth rock felt cool as he made his way through the entrance to the village. Although the tunnel was only 12 feet long, he blinked when he found himself in the sunshine again.

At last Trader arrived in the village. He carried his pack to Kiva Plaza, a large open space where many people of the village were gathered. Old folks sat in the sunshine telling stories. Young women ground corn while others cooked meals. Men sewed clothes from leather hides and made blankets. When they saw Trader, children stopped playing and shouted greetings. Soon a crowd was asking for news from his travels and was wondering what new things he'd brought to trade.

Trader was pleased when East Wind and Blue Corn, his friends from earlier visits, invited him to share a midday meal with their family. There would be plenty of time for trading after the meal.

They walked along the back of the alcove to North Plaza, where East Wind's house was. Here Trader greeted

Balcony House was built onto a narrow ledge only 400 feet long. One end of the ledge came up against a sharp cliff. The other end had a small opening that led to the mesa. The Puebloans built a wall at the narrow opening and a tunnel at the base of this wall. The tunnel—the only way in or out of the village—could be guarded easily.

Corn Woman and the children sitting in the sunny plaza. East Wind and her daughter served roasted deer meat, baked squash, and boiled roots. Best of all was the hot corn bread.

Throughout the meal, Trader talked to East Wind and her family. There was so much news! More turquoise had been discovered far away, and a village to the south had been wiped out by sickness. Another village had reaped a huge crop of corn. Trader warned them of raiding parties from villages where harvests had failed.

East Wind and Blue Corn had news for Trader, too. The piñon nuts were being harvested, an event that hap-

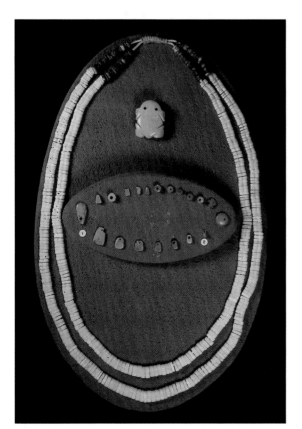

Jade ornaments and jewelry made from seashells were some of the objects traded among the ancient peoples of the region.

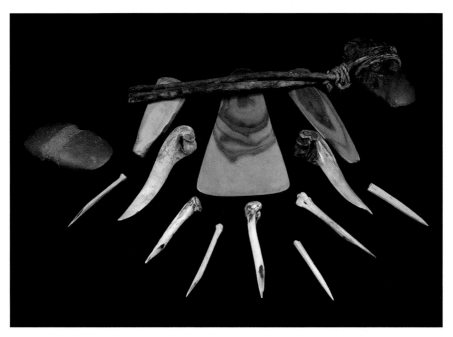

Because local sandstone was too soft to be used for tools, the Puebloans traveled beyond their villages to find harder rock. They commonly shaped animal bones for tools as well.

pened only every two or three years. A woman in the village had given birth to twins. Trader listened carefully. He would carry the news to the other villages he planned to visit before the winter snow came.

Trader finished his large meal and saw that people were looking curiously at his pack. It was time to start trading. He opened his pack and carefully took out his wares. He arranged the salt, turquoise, shells, raw cotton, and copper bells neatly on the ground. The people pressed forward to get a closer look. Many held items they wanted to trade, including blankets made of cotton and of turkey feathers; tools made of sticks, rocks, and bones; and

This double mug may have been used in ceremonies.

assorted goods like stone arrowheads, fine jewelry, and beautiful pottery.

Soon trading began. Someone made an offer, then Trader made a counteroffer. The bargaining went back and forth, back and forth. Finally some agreements were reached. A villager traded a few tools made from bighorn sheep bones for some salt and shells. Another got wonderfully crafted arrows in exchange for a couple of pieces of the beautiful turquoise, which would be made into beads for jewelry. Blue Corn traded a turkey-feather blanket for shiny copper bells and for raw cotton that he'd make into cloth.

Trader had a hard time taking his eyes off the pottery, the finest he had seen. He was glad to make an exchange for a beautiful double mug—a rare vessel made here and at a few other pueblos. Trader also had to have one of the round black-and-white jars to take back to his village. Besides being a thing of beauty, the jar would be very useful. But the woman who'd crafted it seemed reluctant.

How could he get it? He made many fair offers, but she refused them all! Maybe she didn't really want to trade it. Luckily Trader could stay in the village for a few days, giving him time to learn what the woman wanted in exchange for the jar. Without this unique piece, his trip would not be complete. In the meantime, Trader would enjoy the food and the company of the villagers.

Some pottery found at Mesa Verde is ornate and creatively styled, suggesting that making pottery was an art as well as a necessity.

A wall rims Balcony House, which faces eastward and looks over wide Soda Canyon.

On eagle feathers you will fly.
You will bring food,
Food for all the people,
My colored arrows.

—Alice Marriot

With Raven Feather

Ten-year-old Raven Feather walked along the rock wall that formed the front edge of the village, running his fingers against the rough sandstone. He thought of the stories his father had told him of building the wall. Villagers had cut the stones, hammered them to the right size, and rubbed them with other stones to smooth them. Other workers had dug the gray clay from the canyon below. They mixed it with water and ashes to make the mortar that held the stones together.

In the cliffs, the ancient Puebloans found sandstone—a rock that is relatively easy to break apart. Using hammers made of harder kinds of rock, Puebloans cut the sandstone into regular blocks about as long as two adult hands. The bricks were about as wide as a grown-up's palm is long. A mortar of mud, water, and ashes from the fire pits held the blocks together.

Raven Feather watched as a little boy climbed up and stood on top of the three-foot-high wall. A woman nearby shouted a warning at the child, who jumped down safely. Playing on the wall was dangerous. One slip and he would have fallen into the canyon.

Raven Feather looked over the wall and saw the trash littering the slope: old tools, broken pots, cornstalks, animal bones, and ashes from the fire pits. Raven Feather searched with his eyes until he thought he saw the place at the bottom of the canyon where Deer Hunter had been buried. Before his death last winter, Deer Hunter had been a popular old man in the village. He had led the fall hunts and had told the children hunting stories. Raven Feather shivered, remembering how cold it had been then. But fires and blankets made it easy to keep warm indoors.

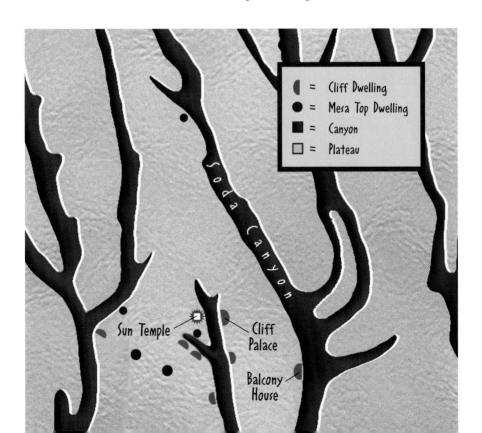

Ancient Puebloans tossed trash—which included food scraps, broken pottery, and used sandals—out the fronts or backs of their houses.

The ancient Puebloans took great care in burying their dead. First they bathed the body and washed the dead person's hair. They put the arms across the chest and tied them in place. Usually they also folded the legs against the body. Then they wrapped the body in a blanket made of cotton and feathers.

When the weather was good, the ancient Puebloans sometimes buried bodies on the mesa or on the floor of the canyons. During the winter, when the ground was frozen, they sometimes dug graves in the soft piles of trash, in unused rooms, and in other sheltered places.

Food and water were placed in the grave with the body. So were personal items, such as tools, bowls, weapons, and jewelry. The ancient Puebloans may have believed that these items helped the person in the afterlife.

The ancient Puebloans built storage units out of stone to keep a supply of precious corn and beans available throughout the winter months. The storage areas had to be carefully sealed off to keep the produce dry and to protect it from being eaten by animals.

Trader certainly brought interesting news, thought Raven Feather. And he'd enjoyed the exciting trading that went on after the meal. Maybe next year, he would have something to trade! His father would teach him to make sewing tools from the bones of bighorn sheep.

But it was time to get back to work. He met Star Gazer, a boy his own age, near the storage rooms. Girls and women squatted in the low-ceilinged rooms, stacking food. Already, carefully arranged piles of dried squash strips sat in the corners, and large heaps of corncobs rose from floor to ceiling. The rooms looked full, but the women managed to pack even more into the small, six-by-six-foot area.

Dried corn leaves, which would keep dampness away from the stored food, crunched beneath their bare feet as Raven Feather and Star Gazer crawled into a storage room. They arranged baskets of beans and shelled corn in stacks that soon reached the ceiling. The boys worked hard but felt proud to be safeguarding the food. There would be enough to feed the village if next year's harvest was bad.

When the storage room was full, the boys pushed a large rock in front of the narrow doorway and then shoved small stones into the openings around the rock. It wasn't long before the storage room was so tightly sealed that not even the smallest rats would be able to crawl in and eat the food.

As soon as the storage room was securely shut, the boys raced through the alcove around the back of the village—speeding past the turkeys searching for food, past

The alcove behind the dwellings at Balcony House must have been a busy place. It was the only way from one end of the village to the other and the only place to fetch water. Cooking fires blackened the alcove's ceiling.

the stench from a garbage heap, and back out to the front of the village. They were going up onto the mesa top.

Raven Feather reached the entry tunnel first and scrambled through. By the time Star Gazer was out of the tunnel, Raven Feather had passed the guard. He scurried up the cliff, expertly using the handholds and footholds. He rested on the ground, listening to his heart pound and watching clouds drift across the blue sky until Star Gazer got to the top of the mesa.

Off they ran, around the sagebrush and past the rabbitbrush with its fading yellow blossoms. Soon they reached the juniper and the piñon pine. Women and children from the village were already at work. Raven Feather saw his mother and sister pulling long strips of bark off the juniper trees. Raven Feather breathed deeply, enjoying the juniper smell. Juniper didn't just have a nice scent. The bark was used for bedding, for mats, and to stuff into

For food, the ancient Puebloans relied on locally grown plants, such as piñon pine trees and juniper bushes.

sandals. The bark could also serve as kindling for fires. Even the berries were useful because they could flavor a meal, be dried and used as beads, or be made into a yellow dye.

Star Gazer joined the children picking the bluish berries from the juniper trees and putting them into baskets. Raven Feather liked picking berries with his friends, but his job today would be more fun than that! The boy expertly climbed the 25-foot-tall trunk of a piñon pine. He braced himself and held onto the trunk with his arms and legs, then began to push and pull. The pressure made the tree sway— only a little bit at first, then more and more. Small, dark nuts fell like rain from the open pinecones. Women and children gathered the nuts and put them into baskets. Later they would shell the nuts to get to the tasty seeds.

The piñon pine *(Pinus edulis)* was a very useful tree. Piñon wood was the main source of firewood and roof timbers. The sticky pitch was chewed, used as glue, and was an ingredient in black dye. It was also spread on skin to treat infected cuts!

The ancient Puebloans not only ate the pine nuts raw, but they ground some into an oily paste to eat with corn bread.

As Raven Feather climbed down the tree, he felt something sticky on his hand. It was the yellowish pitch (sap) from the tree. Raven Feather found the spot on the tree where the pitch had gathered and pulled off a small piece to chew.

After a few hours, the baskets were full of piñon nuts and juniper berries. Raven Feather and Star Gazer began to lug heavy baskets back to the village. Raven Feather stopped and listened to the sound of quiet footsteps coming nearer and nearer. He remembered Trader's warnings about dangerous raiding parties from other villages. The boy motioned to his friend to be quiet. Both boys were relieved to see that it was only Cold Rain, a hunter from

A hunter with a bow and arrow scans the mesa for deer or bighorn sheep.

Balcony House, carrying a bow and a pouch with arrows in it.

The pair watched Cold Rain pass. Raven Feather could hear the man singing a hunting song. The boy knew the hunter carried prayer sticks. Cold Rain probably also had a small stone or clay image of an animal that was a good hunter.

Raven Feather thought about the things that hunters needed to know—where to find the trails and waterholes the animals used, and what was the best way to track each animal. A hunter needed to have patience and to have skill with different weapons. Last summer Raven Feather, Star Gazer, Light Cloud, and other village children had scared deer from the fields. That had been fun, but it wasn't like hunting. Raven Feather knew that he had a lot to learn before he could be a hunter.

Although it looked like Cold Rain was going hunting alone, Raven Feather knew that hunters also worked in groups. He had seen the hunters form a long line across the mesa and walk closer and closer to the edge of the cliff. Frightened animals, including deer, had run away from the hunters and had become trapped between the men and the edge of the mesa. Then the hunters had killed some of the trapped animals with arrows. Later the men tanned the hides into leather and used the bones to make tools. Everyone shared the delicious meat.

Raven Feather and Star Gazer walked across the mesa toward Balcony House. They passed other hunters, some from their village, some from other villages. The men all looked brave and strong. Raven Feather looked forward to the time when he would be a hunter.

The Sun Temple sprawled on top of the mesa. The building had no roof so visitors had an excellent view of the sky.

...the kiva was a place of consciousness between heaven and earth where the past, present, and eternity merged. —Sylvio Acatos

With Great Cloud

Great Cloud, the priest from Balcony House, stood in a small, roofless room at the Sun Temple. He watched the sky darken. The moon, low on the horizon, shone huge and white. Soon it would be night.

Priests, or holy men, from nearby villages filled the Sun Temple, a large D-shaped structure built on top of the mesa. Great Cloud and the other priests were planning a celebration of the harvest that would include chanting, drumming, dancing, and feasting.

When the meeting ended, Great Cloud and the others climbed a wooden ladder to exit the doorless room. All stepped off onto the thick wall separating the rooms. As he walked along the tops of the walls, Great Cloud looked to the west. The sky was slowly filling with colors—red, yellow, pink, and orange—as the sun slipped below the horizon. The Sun Temple was Great Cloud's favorite place. When he

49

was younger, he had helped build it. These days younger people continued the construction. Great Cloud had also labored on Balcony House. It had been hard work, but he was glad to live in the cliff village instead of up on the mesa.

After climbing down from the walls, Great Cloud saw Fast River, the young man he was teaching to be a priest.

Experts believe that ancient Puebloans from many Mesa Verde villages built the Sun Temple. The priests may have believed that the people needed a place to worship and to celebrate together.

The stone building is 122 feet long, 73 feet wide, and one story high. It has 24 rooms, including three kivas and one plaza.

The Sun Temple is a roofless building open to the sun and weather. Scientists believe that the ancient Puebloans had religious reasons for this design. Because some of the rooms have no doors, visitors must walk along the tops of the walls and climb down ladders to enter.

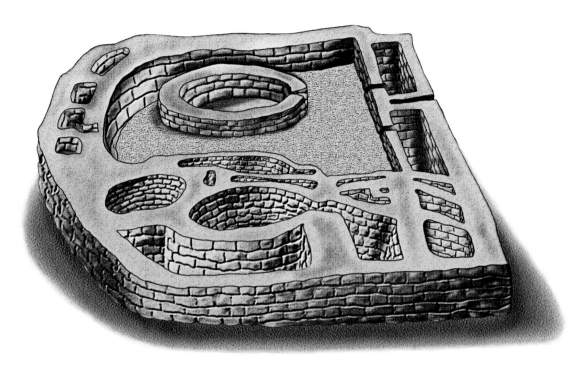

The careful construction of the Sun Temple was never finished.

The two men said good-bye to the other priests and began walking back to Balcony House. As they walked, Great Cloud spoke. There was so much to pass on—legends, rituals, medicines, and chants.

Great Cloud slowly climbed down the cliff face to the ledge leading to Balcony House. It tired him out. He was glad to pass the guards and crawl through the tunnel to enter the village. After emerging from the tunnel, he stood slowly and rubbed his aching knees. Although he loved the Sun Temple, it was nice to come home. The moon cast a strong, silvery light that made it easy to see where he was going. People huddled in small groups around fires in Kiva Plaza. Some sang songs, others gambled, and some were talking quietly together. Great Cloud and Fast River heard chanting rising from the first kiva.

The elderly priest took a deep breath and looked up at the stars. He walked to the center of the courtyard where a ladder rose through the kiva's smoke hole. He climbed down the ladder, coughing in the smoky air. A small fire illuminated the priests and boys sitting on the benches that lined the room. Shadows danced on the walls around them.

The chanting ended soon after Fast River followed Great Cloud into the kiva. One of the priests began a story about Mother Earth, the origin of all life. Great Cloud was pleased to see that Fast River had an interested look on his face. As a priest, Fast River would need to know all of the legends.

Great Cloud looked around the room at the faces of the men, both young and old. He pulled a turkey-feather blanket up around his shoulders and listened to the story.

Except for a hole in the plaza floor and protruding ladders, kivas were all but invisible to the ancient Puebloans.

Kivas are circular pits, usually 12 to 14 feet in diameter (the width of the circle) and 7 to 8 feet deep. The Puebloans had dug two kivas at Balcony House from the layers of rubble that made the alcove floor level. Sturdy brick sides supported the roof, which seemed like part of the plaza floor. Made of logs with layers of clay and dirt, these roofs helped make the kivas secret places.

A ladder poked through the smoke hole in the roof, allowing people to climb in and smoke to escape. Air from outside blew down a narrow shaft, forcing out the smoke from the crackling fire (usually in a pit near the center of the room). A stone, called a deflector, protected the fire and helped spread the fresh air through the small room.

Each kiva had a *sipapu* in its floor. About three inches in diameter and three inches deep, a sipapu may have symbolized an entrance to the spirit world. The ancient Puebloans may have believed that their gods lived underground. Although no one knows for sure, many scientists believe that kivas were religious places where priests gathered. Other experts guess that kivas might have functioned as meeting places or as underground kitchens.

Changes in growing conditions may have caused a food shortage that made life tough for the ancient Puebloans.

*We have lived upon this land from days
beyond history's records, far past any living
memory, deep in the time of legend.*

—A Taos Pueblo man quoted by Alfonso Ortiz

Afterword

People lived in the cliff villages for another few decades. By 1300—only 50 years after this story takes place—hardly anyone inhabited Mesa Verde. Yucca sandals, corncobs, and baskets had been left behind. Archaeologists still find beautiful jars hidden behind rocks, as though someone planned to come back and get them. But no one ever did.

Why did the ancient Puebloans leave? Why didn't they come back? Just as no one knows why some ancient Puebloans left villages on the mesa for the cliffs, no one is certain why they left the cliffs. Most likely, it was a combination of many different things. The land might not have been good for growing crops anymore. Animals may have been hunted away. Scientists know that the changing climate shortened the growing season. Research shows that a period of drought, lasting from 1273 to 1299, made water scarce. So there was less food and water, but the population may have been growing.

Ancient Puebloans left behind clues to their way of life, such as pottery, tools, food, weapons, and clothes.

Having more people to feed and less food to eat could have caused lots of problems. People may have starved, and wars over stored grain could have started. Maybe people worried that their religion had failed them or that their gods were angry. Disease—which could spread rapidly in the crowded, isolated communities—might have killed many people. A new religion may have lured people south. Wars between villages may have made people scared and unhappy. They may have wanted to leave their troubles behind.

Whatever the reason, after leaving their homes at Mesa Verde, the ancient Puebloans moved southward into the lands that would become New Mexico, Arizona, and Texas—where some modern Pueblo people live. The Hopi, the Tewa, and the Zuni trace their nations back to the ancient people of Mesa Verde.

Mesa Verde was deserted for nearly 700 years. Over time some of the buildings collapsed. Dirt drifted into springs, and weeds took root in the soil. Handholds and toeholds eroded. Trees and shrubs grew in fields on the mesa. The Navaho—Native Americans who moved into the area around the year 1500—avoided the deserted towns. Spanish explorers passed near Mesa Verde but did not go onto the mesa.

Over centuries the structures of Mesa Verde villages collapsed. Some rooms filled with rubble, and erosion ate away at others.

The Weatherill brothers, self-taught archaeologists, rediscovered and explored ancient Puebloan structures across the region.

When the Mesa Verde area became part of the United States in 1848, the land became available to white settlers. Miners came looking for gold and silver. One miner took the first photographs of the dwellings in 1874. In the late 1870s, Balcony House was rediscovered by a white settler. In 1881 cattle ranchers came across Cliff Palace as they searched for some of their cows during a snowstorm. The ranchers, the Wetherill brothers, found hundreds of sites in the area. As word spread about the cliff pueblos, more people came to Mesa Verde. Many visitors took away important artifacts. In 1906 the U.S. government created a national park at Mesa Verde to protect the area and to allow scientists to study it.

Scientists have learned many things about the ancient Puebloans by investigating Mesa Verde. The careful study of graves has revealed the height, lifespan, and general health of the ancient Puebloans. Houses, tools, and jewelry have yielded valuable information about how the ancient Puebloans lived, worked, and crafted goods. Manos, metates, and storage rooms full of dried corn teach scientists how and what Puebloans ate. Other experts study the beautiful pottery that the ancient Puebloans left behind.

But many mysteries remain. Ancient Puebloan lifestyles, beliefs, and ceremonies are unknown. Scientists can't read the petroglyphs (carvings on rock) on walls and other spots. No one knows if the people were peaceful or warlike. The modern Pueblo peoples may have cultures like those of their ancestors, but many things can change in 700 years!

Scientists have worked hard at Mesa Verde to restore and preserve the dwellings. They have reconstructed kivas, rebuilt balconies, leveled floors, and stabilized some walls with metal braces.

In restoring the ancient villages, builders placed metal braces in walls to steady the precarious structures.

Nearly a million people from all over the world visit Mesa Verde National Park each year. They tour the cliff dwellings, including Balcony House, and view pottery and tools made by the ancient Puebloans. Visitors get a rare glimpse at the world of the fascinating people who once made this area their home.

Visitors to Mesa Verde National Park can learn what life may have been like for the ancient cliff dwellers.

Glossary

ancient Puebloans: The Native Americans who lived in the southwestern region of what would become the United States. Many different groups of people are considered to be ancient Puebloans, including the Hohokam and the Mogollon. In this story, the term refers to the people who lived at Mesa Verde in the 1200s.

metate: This Spanish word describes a flat stone, often with a trough or high sides. Corn kernels are placed on the metate and rubbed with another stone, called a *mano,* to grind the kernels into cornmeal.

plaza: A paved public area surrounded on some sides by buildings.

sandstone cliff: A steep, rocky slope of sedimentary rock made up of sand cemented together by minerals.

Pronunciation Guide

adobe	ah-DOH-bee
kiva	KEE-vah
mano	MAH-no
Mesa Verde	MAY-sah VAYR-day
metate	may-TAH-tay
piñon	PIN-yuhn
Puebloan	PWEH-bloh-ahn
sipapu	SEE-pah-poo

Further Reading

Arnold, Caroline. *The Ancient Cliff Dwellers of Mesa Verde*. New York: Clarion Books, 1992.

Bledsoe, Sara. *Colorado*. Minneapolis: Lerner Publications Company, 1993.

Brody, J.J. *A Day With a Mimbres*. Minneapolis: Runestone Press, 1999.

Cory, Steven. *Pueblo Indian*. Minneapolis: Lerner Publications Company, 1996.

Naranjo, Tito E. *A Day With a Pueblo*. Minneapolis: Runestone Press, 1999.

Powell, Susan. *The Pueblos*. New York: Franklin Watts, 1993.

Touring Information

Mesa Verde National Park is open year-round, but most sites can only be toured in the summer months. Guides give tours of Balcony House between May and October. For more information about visiting Mesa Verde,

write to:
Mesa Verde National Park
P.O. Box 8
Mesa Verde National Park, CO 81330

or call:
(970) 529-4475

or visit the website at:
http://www.mesaverde.org

Index

About the Author

Robert Young, a prolific author of children's books, created the *How It Was* series to enable readers to tour famous landmarks through the experiences of people who did or may have lived, worked, or visited there. Robert, who makes his home in Eugene, Oregon, teaches elementary school and visits schools around the country to talk with students about writing and curiosity. Among his other literary credits are *Money* and *Game Day*, titles published by Carolrhoda Books, Inc.

Acknowledgments

For quoted material: p. 5, Jennings, Heather, *In Search of Ancient North America* (New York: John Wiley & Sons, Inc., 1996); p. 11, Pike, Donald G., *Anasazi, Ancient People of the Rock* (New York: Crown Publishers, Inc., 1974); p. 21, Cory, Steven, *Pueblo Indian* (Minneapolis: Lerner Publications, 1996); p. 29, Marriot, Alice, *Indians of the Four Corners* (Santa Fe: Ancient City Press, 1992); p. 39, Marriot, Alice, *Indians;* p. 48, Acatos, Sylvio, *Pueblos: Prehistoric Indian Cultures of the Southwest* (New York: Facts on File, Inc., 1990); p. 54, Jennings, Francis, *The Founders of America* (New York: W.W. Norton & Company, Inc., 1993).
For photos and artwork: National Park Service/Mesa Verde National Park, pp. 1, 15 (both), 17 [neg. # 4635], 48, 57, 58; Buddy Mays/TRAVEL STOCK, pp. 4, 19, 42; © Jack Olson, pp. 6, 50 (right), 56; © Robert Winslow, pp. 8, 9, 10, 23 (inset), 33, 38, 43, 59, 60; © Chuck Place, p. 12; Paula Jansen, pp. 16, 44 (right); Mesa Verde Museum Association, Inc., pp. 18, 41; © Paul Myers, pp. 20, 23 (left), 35, 36; © North Wind Pictures, pp. 26, 32, 46; © Robert E. Barber, pp. 27, 28, 30; © Gilbert R. Wenger, courtesy of the Mesa Verde Museum Association, pp. 34, 44 (left), 53, 54; courtesy, Colorado Historical Society, p. 37; © James P. Rowan, pp. 50 (inset), 52; All maps and artwork by Lejla Fazlic Omerovic. Cover: © Robert Winslow.